TWEETABLE
BILL CLINTON

Infotainment Press

Tweetable Bill Clinton: Quips, Quotes & Other One-Liners

Copyright © 2021 by Infotainment Press

All rights reserved. No portion of this book may be reproduced, stored in a retrieval system, or transmitted in any form or by any means—electronic, mechanical, photocopy, recording, scanning, or other—except for brief quotations in critical reviews or articles, without the prior written permission of the publisher.

All quotes in this book are derived from speeches given by the author while he served as President of the United States.

TWEETABLE
BILL CLINTON

QUIPS, QUOTES & OTHER ONE-LINERS

All over the world . . . people still look to us and trust us to help them seek the blessings of peace and freedom.

We don't need a constitutional amendment; we need action.

To make the American dream achievable for all, we must make college affordable for all.

Nothing good ever came of hate.

I believe that in millions and millions of different ways, our entire country is reasserting our commitment to the bedrock values.

*I*f we want America to lead, we've got to set a good example.

*W*e need a 21st-century revolution in education, guided by our faith that every single child can learn.

*T*his must be a campaign of ideas, not a campaign of insults. The American people deserve it.

We have a government . . . that is a progressive instrument of the common good, rooted in our oldest values.

Opportunity alone is not enough.

We must provide for our nation the way a family provides for its children.

People who work hard still need support to get ahead in the new economy.

America became the world's mightiest industrial power.

Great rewards will come to those who can live together, learn together, work together, forge new ties that bind together.

Our open, creative society stands to benefit more than any other if we understand and act on the realities of interdependence.

The challenge of our past remains the challenge of our future: will we be one nation, one people, with one common destiny?

It is time for Americans to put a new Africa on our map.

The greatest untapped market for American enterprise is right here in America.

We must fight against [abiding bigotry and intolerance], in our country and in our hearts.

Discrimination is not just morally wrong, it hurts everybody.

We are helping to win an unrivaled peace and prosperity all across the world.

The point is not to put our children down but to lift them up.

We have seen the terrible, terrible price that people pay when they insist on fighting and killing their neighbors.

Old habits and thinking patterns are deeply ingrained and die hard.

*W*e are reminded of the capacity
for people everywhere . . .
to slip into pure evil.

Affirmative action has been good for America.

Because previous generations of Americans stood up for freedom . . . the American people are more secure and more prosperous.

Our country is still the strongest force for peace and freedom on Earth.

We have grown into an experiment in democratic diversity fueled by openness and promise.

Every day and every individual is a precious opportunity.

Taking reasonable risks for peace keeps us from being drawn into far more costly conflicts later.

We must not let . . . confidence drift into complacency.

You must not allow the ship of peace to sink on the rocks of old habits and hard grudges.

We need a new government . . . humble enough not to try to solve all our problems for us.

Anyone who takes on our troops will suffer the consequences. We will fight fire with fire and then some.

The promise of our future is limitless.

Our civil life is suffering in America today.

From our birth, America has always been more than just a place.

The 20th century is ending not with helpless indignation but with a hopeful affirmation of human dignity and human rights.

Our individual dreams must be realized by our common efforts.

The search for common ground demands the courage of an open mind.

History has shown us that you can't allow the mass extermination of people, and just sit by and watch it happen.

The state of our Union is the strongest it has ever been.

When divisions have threatened to bring our house down, somehow we have always moved together to shore it up.

America is far more than a place. It is an idea, the most powerful idea in the history of nations.

All the world's wealth and a thousand armies are no match for the strength and decency of the human spirit.

We also have got to do our part in the global endeavor to reduce the debts of the poorest countries.

The global economy requires us to seek opportunity not just at home but in all the markets of the world.

My fellow Americans, I stand before you tonight to report that the state of our Union is strong.

*T*he urgent question of our time is whether we can make Change our friend and not our enemy.

White racism may be black people's burden, but it's white people's problem.

The American people look at their capital, and they see a city where the well-connected and the well-protected can work the system.

Our country is and always has been a great and good nation. But the best is yet to come if we all do our parts.

Democracy must have prosperity.

Those who do show the courage to break with the past are entitled to their stake in the future.

Quietly, but with gathering force, the ground has shifted beneath our feet as we have moved into an information age.

Abortion should not only be safe and legal, it should be rare.

We will be held to a high standard, indeed, because our chance to do good is so great.

It is the power of our ideas . . . that makes America a uniquely trusted nation.

The promise of America was born in the 18th century out of the bold conviction that we are all created equal.

Our children need and deserve a peaceful, stable, free Europe.

There will be no progress in the absence of real responsibility on the part of all Americans.

America was built on challenges, not promises.

There is only so much temptation some people can stand when they turn up against a brick wall day after day after day.

We need a new government . . . strong enough to give us the tools to solve our problems for ourselves.

In our national community we're all different; we're all the same.

We want to live forever, and we're getting there.

How do we make the American dream of opportunity for all a reality for all Americans who are willing to work for it?

This is, after all, a very great country. And we have become great by what we have overcome.

We know we can become stronger if we bridge our differences.

We need a new sense of responsibility for
   a new century.

As long as our dreams outweigh our memories,
   America will be forever young. That is our destiny.
   And this is our moment.

Let all of us who want to stand up against racism
   do our part to roll back the divide.

A nation that lives as a community must value all
   its communities.

We cannot stop all war for all time, but we can stop some wars.

We are fortunate to be alive at this moment in history.

Voices of isolation say America should retreat from its responsibilities. I say they are wrong.

Because of American leadership, more people than ever before live free and at peace.

There will always be those who define the worth of their lives . . . not by what they're for but by what they are against.

Africa is mankind's first home.

Every dollar we devote to preventing conflicts . . .
   brings a sure return in security and savings.

We must maintain a strong and ready military.

Prejudice and contempt cripple both those who hate
   and those who are hated, robbing both of what they
   might become.

We can meet all the other challenges if we can go forward as One America.

If we do not act, the moment will pass, and we will lose the best possibilities of our future.

To bring our people together we must openly and honestly deal with the issues that divide us.

Our bridge to the future must include bridges to other nations.

Already we have dismantled many of the blocks and barriers that divided our parents' world.

The lesson of our history . . . is that great goals are reached step by step, always building on our progress.

I still believe in a place called Hope, a place called America.

We should do more to help Americans help each other.

The single greatest difference between war and peace is that in peace, everybody can win.

We must embrace boldly and resolutely that duty to lead.

Laws alone do not change society.

Our democracy must be not only the envy of the world but the engine of our own renewal.

We cannot empower all Americans by a simple strategy of taking opportunity away from some Americans.

All Americans have not just a right but a solemn responsibility to rise as far as their talents and determination can take them.

How do we preserve our old and enduring values as we move into the future?

Blacks must understand and acknowledge the roots of white fear in America.

We must go forward as one America, one nation working together to meet the challenges we face together.

Our people have always mustered the determination to construct from crises the pillars of our history.

We must clean the house of white America of racism.

Fellow citizens, let us build a nation ever moving forward toward realizing the full potential of all its citizens.

I really believe we're on the verge of the most exciting period in human history.

We can't reward work and family unless men and women get equal pay for equal work.

The enduring worth of our nation lies in our shared values and our soaring spirit.

Opportunity and responsibility: They go hand in hand. We can't have one without the other.

Change is not always easy, but we have to decide whether we're going to try to hold it back . . . or reap its benefits.

The voice of the people will always speak louder than the din of narrow interests.

By expanding trade, we can advance the cause of freedom and democracy around the world.

Let us put our country first, remembering that regardless of party label, we are all Americans.

We must master the forces of change in the world and keep American leadership strong and sure for an uncharted time.

We must be shapers of events, not observers.

Now each of us must hold high the torch of citizenship in our own lives.

African-Americans have lived too long with a justice system that in too many cases has been and continues to be less than just.

The European Union and the United States must plan for tomorrow, not just today.

Firmness can stop armies and save lives.

Our purpose must be to bring together the world around freedom and democracy and peace, and to oppose those who would tear it apart.

I must take complete responsibility for all my actions, both public and private.

We all want our children to grow up in a world where their talents are matched by their opportunities.

Whether we like it or not . . . the world's economies are more and more interconnected and interdependent.

Too many destructive ideas are gaining currency in our midst.

I know I speak for everyone when I say to Saddam Hussein, "You cannot defy the will of the world."

We cannot, we will not, succumb to the dark impulses that lurk in the far regions of the soul everywhere.

The rising tide is not lifting all boats.

When we set up this country, abuse of people by Government was a big problem.

It is the right thing to do for all the rest of us to see that everybody has a chance.

The world is no longer divided into two hostile camps.

We need not shrink from the challenge of the global economy.

America must stand against the poisoned appeals of extreme nationalism.

Wherever people of all races and backgrounds come together in a shared endeavor and get a fair chance, we do just fine.

I love and revere the rich and proud history of America.

America stands alone as the world's indispensable nation.

We must learn to live in harmony with other species.

I challenge America's families to work harder to stay together.

The values that used to hold us all together seem to be coming apart.

Where it can give Americans the power to make a real difference in their everyday lives, government should do more, not less.

Though our challenges are fearsome, so are our strengths.

My fellow Americans, you, too, must play your part in our renewal.

You must draw strength from the past and energy from the promise of a new future.

The era of big government is over. But we can't go back to the era of fending for yourself.

[T]here is a] line between those who confront every day with a clenched fist and those who confront every day with an open hand.

Anyone who has committed an act of domestic violence against a spouse or a child should not buy a gun.

No tie binds different people together like citizen service.

We act to stand united with our allies for peace.

We cannot become the world's policeman, but where our values and our interests are at stake . . . we must act.

Like every taxpayer, I'm outraged by the reports of abuses by the IRS.

Our communities are only as healthy as the air our children breathe, the water they drink, the Earth they will inherit.

Even Presidents have private lives.

We must reach beyond our fears and our divisions to a new time of great and common purpose.

When America does not lead, the consequences can be very grave, not only for others but eventually for us as well.

Allies who share our goals can also share our burdens.

Now is the moment for this generation to meet our historic responsibility to the 21st century.

Peace must be waged with a warrior's resolve: bravely, proudly, and relentlessly.

The threats we face today as Americans respect no nation's borders.

Discrimination against any American is un-American.

I'll leave the Presidency more idealistic, more full of hope than the day I arrived.

Whether we like it or not, we are one nation, one family, indivisible. And for us, divorce or separation are not options.

Make no mistake about it, today's possibilities are not tomorrow's guarantees.

There is a power in freedom that you cannot underestimate. We take it for granted.

When a people are singled out for destruction because of their heritage and faith . . . the world will not look the other way.

I came to this hallowed chamber on a mission, to restore the American dream for all our people

We live in an age of possibility.

Medical decisions ought to be made by medical doctors, not insurance company accountants.

Race is not about government or political leaders, it is about what is in the heart and minds and life of the American people.

The promise we sought in a new land we will find again in a land of new promise.

No good house was ever built on a bad foundation.

Terrorists are as big a threat to our future, perhaps bigger, than organized crime.

Building a family is the hardest job a man can do, but it's also the most important.

We cannot save all the world's children, but we can save many of them.

We can and should be the world's very best
    peacemaker.

I have steered my course by our enduring values:
    opportunity for all, responsibility from all,
    a community of all Americans.

Prejudice and contempt, cloaked in the pretense of
    religious or political conviction, are no different.

The new promise of the global economy,
    the information age . . . all these are ours to seize.

We are the world's most diverse democracy, and the world looks to us to show that it is possible to live and advance together.

We know we have to face hard truths and take strong steps. But we have not done so.

So let us challenge ourselves to build a world in which no branch of humanity is again threatened with destruction.

All Americans have not just a right but a solemn responsibility to give something back to their communities and their country.

Citizen service is an American responsibility which all Americans should embrace.

Let us shape the hope of this day into the noblest chapter in our history.

Prejudice and contempt have nearly destroyed our nation in the past. They plague us still. They fuel the fanaticism of terror.

We must be now, as we were in the beginning, a new nation.

Before us we can see even greater, grander frontiers of possibility.

We have achieved a victory for a safer world, for our democratic values, and for a stronger America.

A good society honors its entire family.

We all cherish family and faith, freedom and responsibility.

The preeminent mission of our new government is to give all Americans an opportunity . . . to build better lives.

America reached out across the globe to millions who, like us, longed for the blessings of liberty.

Together with our friends and allies, we will work to shape change, lest it engulf us.

Just as peace has its pioneers, peace will always have its rivals.

We will stand mighty for peace and freedom, and maintain a strong defense against terror and destruction.

We must move strongly against new threats to our security.

There are places in our country where the free enterprise system simply doesn't reach.

On the forge of common enterprise, Americans of all backgrounds can hammer out a common identity.

We have seen America pay a terrible price for any form of discrimination.

There is a line between those who look to the future and those who cling to the past.

While we honor the past, let us imagine the future.

I am determined to take our best traditions into the future.

Let us have faith, American faith that we are not leaving our greatness behind.

We can only achieve our destiny together; one hand, one generation, one American connecting to another.

We should begin this new century by honoring our historic responsibility to empower the first Americans.

I challenge a new generation of young Americans to a season of service; to act on your idealism.

The greatest progress we have made, and the greatest progress we have yet to make, is in the human heart.

America is a strong force for peace.

We are on the right track to the 21st century.

Only you can decide between division and unity, between hard lives and high hopes.

Not a single American family should ever have to choose between the job they need and the child they love.

The greatest environmental challenge of the new century is global warming.

America, we must clean our house of racism.

Today, because of our dedication, America's ideals are more and more the aspirations of people everywhere in the world.

Rarely have Americans lived through so much change in so many ways in so short a time.

We are winning back our optimism, the enduring faith that we can master any difficulty.

We have seen us grow stronger as we have steadily let more and more of our hatreds and our fears go.

Our world leadership grows out of the power of our example here at home, out of our ability to remain strong as one America.

Education must be our Nation's highest priority.

We must bring to our task today the vision and will of those who came before us.

Our Founders saw themselves in the light of posterity. We can do no less.

Most Americans live near a community college. The roads that take them there can be paths to a better future.

America has always sought and always risen to every challenge.

We must renew our commitment to America's diplomacy.

We still haven't learned to talk frankly, to listen carefully, and to work together across racial lines.

Drugs are deadly; drugs are wrong; drugs can cost you your life.

People on every continent can look to us and see the reflection of their own great potential.

Our greatest responsibility is to embrace a new spirit of community for a new century.

We must all take responsibility
for ourselves, our conduct,
and our attitudes.

We must work together, learn together, live together, serve together.

In the choice between peace and war, America must choose peace.

There is nothing wrong with America that cannot be cured by what is right with America.

We should not tax middle-income Americans for the money they spend on college.

By our dreams and labors we will redeem the promise of America in the 21st century.

White America must understand and acknowledge the roots of black pain.

Martin Luther King's dream was the American Dream. His quest is our quest.

Clearly America must continue to lead the world we did so much to make.

As times change, so government must change.

It's long past time to make good on our debt to the United Nations.

When we allow people to pit us against one another or spend energy denying opportunity . . . everyone is held back.

Problems that once seemed destined to deepen now bend to our efforts.

Globalization is about more than economics.

We need a Europe that is coming together, not falling apart.

I challenge our parents to become their children's first teachers.

The job of ending discrimination in this country is not over.

In a truly open market, we can out-compete anyone, anywhere on Earth.

We achieve our aims by defending our values and leading the forces of freedom and peace.

The flame of our Statue of Liberty will always burn brighter than the fires that burn our churches . . . synagogues . . . mosques.

When a child is gunned down on a street in the Bronx, no matter what our race, he is our American child.

Our leadership in the world is strong, bringing hope for new peace.

Inaction in the face of brutality simply invites more brutality.

When we give all Americans a chance to be full partners in our common enterprise, then everybody is pushed forward.

Can we hope not just to follow, but even to surpass the achievements of the 20th century in America?

We should look out for the interests of ordinary people.

We must be committed to the pursuit of opportunity for all Americans.

Surely, there will come a time when everywhere reconciliation will replace recrimination.

It takes courage to let go of familiar divisions. It takes faith to walk down a new road.

We should, all of us, be filled with gratitude and humility for our present progress and prosperity.

If we have stronger families, we will have a stronger America.

We must work harder to overcome our differences, in our hearts and in our laws.

The question is no longer who's to blame but what to do.

Let the final test of everything we do be a simple one: Is it good for the American people?

The world's greatest democracy will lead a whole world of democracies.

None of us would be here tonight if it weren't for our teachers. We ought to lift them up, not tear them down.

You can't gain ground if you're standing still.

We must combat an unholy axis of new threats from terrorists, international criminals, and drug traffickers.

We must preserve the magnificent natural environment that is left.

Government is not the problem, and government is not the solution. We—the American people—we are the solution.

We cannot influence other countries' decisions if we send them a message that we're backing away from trade with them.

It turns out giving everybody a chance, not a guarantee but a chance, is good for the rest of us.

Differences of opinion rooted in different experiences are healthy, indeed essential, for democracies.

We will never be what we ought to be if we allow our country to be led by those who believe we are better off on our own.

If America is going to be prosperous and secure, we need a Europe that is prosperous, secure, undivided, and free.

We have all seen what happens when guns fall into the wrong hands.

We cannot change the past, but we can and must do everything in our power to help build a future without fear and full of hope.

The Government must become a better partner for people in places in urban and rural America that are caught in poverty.

To renew America, we must meet challenges abroad as well at home.

We must be bound together by a faith more powerful than any doctrine that divides us.

We have the power and the duty to
   build a new era of peace and security.

America has a responsibility to stand with our allies when they are trying to save innocent lives and preserve peace.

The enemy of our time is inaction.

We still have too many Americans who give in to their fears of those who are different from them.

Let's never, ever shut the federal government down again.

Think of all the innocent people who died in this bloody century because democracies reacted too late to evil and aggression.

We have an obligation . . . to leave our children a legacy of opportunity, not a legacy of debt.

Let us put aside personal advantage so that we can feel the pain and see the promise of America.

I never told anybody to lie, not a single time—never.

Self-reliance and teamwork are not opposing virtues; we must have both.

Let us resolve to reform our politics, so that power and privilege no longer shout down the voice of the people.

White Americans and black Americans often see the same world in drastically different ways.

We must shape this global economy, not shrink from it.

Long before we were so diverse, our Nation's motto was *E pluribus unum*: out of many, we are one.

We have stood up for peace and freedom because it's in our interest to do so and because it is the right thing to do.

The rift between blacks and whites exists still in a very special way in America.

None of us can finish the race alone.

There is no longer division between what is foreign and what is domestic; the world economy, the environment . . . they affect us.

We must allow democracy and prosperity to take root without violence.

An isolated China is not good for America; a China playing its proper role in the world is.

Our economic revolution has been matched by a revival of the American spirit.

We cannot restore economic opportunity or solve our social problems unless we find a way to bring the American people together.

To renew America, we must revitalize our democracy.

Affirmative action did not cause the great economic problems of the American middle class.

Let us work together as a community of civilized nations to strengthen our ability to prevent and, if necessary, to stop genocide.

We must ask more of ourselves, we
must expect more of each other, and
we must face our challenges together.

We must not be isolationist. We must not be the world's policeman.

A big part of peace is children growing up safely, learning together, and growing together.

The chain of peace that protects us grows stronger with every new link that is forged.

It is beyond wrong when law-abiding black parents have to tell their law-abiding children to fear the police.

An economic crisis anywhere can affect economies everywhere.

We cannot accept a world in which part of humanity lives on the cutting edge . . . and the rest live on the edge of survival.

I am hopeful about America.

Passing a law, even the best possible law, is only a first step. The next step is to make it work.

We need partners to deepen the meaning of democracy in America.

Community means living by the defining American value, the ideal heard 'round the world that we are all created equal.

Everyone knows elections have become too expensive, fueling a fundraising arms race.

In this new era there are still times when America and America alone can and should make the difference for peace.

We cannot expect our children to raise themselves up in schools that are literally falling down.

Family is the foundation of American life.

We earn our livelihood in peaceful competition with people all across the earth.

With a vast new century stretching before us we know that the world is changing in ways we cannot fully understand.

The challenge of our past remains the challenge of our future: Will we all come together, or come apart?

Every day democracy must be defended and a more perfect union can always lie ahead.

Our greatest strength is the power of our ideas, which are still new in many lands.

I have had to finally put to rest the bogus idea that you cannot grow the economy and protect the environment at the same time.

In a little more than 50 years, there will be no majority race in America.

We may not share a common past, but we surely do share a common future.

Each and every one of us, in our own way, must assume personal responsibility for our neighbors and our nation.

The American people must prosper in the global economy.

*W*e need a new government that is smaller, lives within its means, and does more with less.

We should do more than just tolerate our diversity; we should honor it and celebrate it.

Let us build a bridge wide enough and strong enough for every American to cross over to a blessed land of new promise.

We must make the basic bargain of opportunity and responsibility available to all Americans, not just a few.

I'm having to become quite an expert in this business of asking for forgiveness.

The preservation of our liberty and our union depends upon responsible citizenship.

As we become ever more diverse, we must work harder to unite around our common values and our common humanity.

We must teach our children to be good citizens.

I am convinced that the dangers of acting are far outweighed by the dangers of not acting.

By acting now, we are upholding our values, protecting our interests, and advancing the cause of peace.

There will always be those who define the worth of their lives not by who they are but by who they aren't.

Democracy requires human rights for everyone, everywhere.

A strong nation rests on the rock of responsibility.

This moment in which the racial divide is so clearly out in the open need not be a setback for us.

When a woman dies from a beating, no matter what our race or hers, she is our American sister.

Problems that start beyond our borders can quickly become problems within them.

America has always been freedom's greatest champion.

We do not need to build a bridge to the past. We need to build a bridge to the future.

This global gap requires more than compassion; it requires action.

Our hopes, our hearts, our hands, are with those on every continent who are building democracy and freedom.

Yesterday is yesterday. If we try to recapture it, we will only lose tomorrow.

We must exercise responsibility not just at home
	but around the world.

The spirit we bring to our work will make
	all the difference.

As we demand more from our schools,
	we should also invest more in our schools.

Our culture lives in every community, and every
	community has places of historic value that tell
	our stories as Americans.

Where our interests are at stake and we can make a difference, we should be, and we must be, peacemakers.

I'll leave the Presidency more confident than ever that America's best days lie ahead.

When America's partnerships are weak and our leadership is in doubt, it undermines our ability to secure our interests.

This is not a Democratic or a Republican issue. Giving people a chance to live their dreams is an American issue.

Once-bitter foes are clasping hands and changing history, and long-suffering people are moving closer to normal lives.

A society rooted in responsibility must first promote the value of work, not welfare.

In serving, we recognize a simple but powerful truth: we need each other. And we must care for one another.

Every time drugs course through the vein of another child, it clouds the future of all our American children.

Let us do what it takes to remain the indispensable nation, to keep America strong, secure, and prosperous.

If we're going to empower America, we have to do more than talk about it.

There are times and places where our leadership can mean the difference between peace and war.

We must do what America does best: offer more opportunity to all and demand responsibility from all.

You have the right to know all your medical options, not just the cheapest.

Our Founders set America on a permanent course toward a more perfect Union.

The journey of our America must go on.

Education is more than ever the key to our children's future; we must make sure all our children have that key.

We must never, ever believe that our diversity is a weakness. It is our greatest strength.

Profound and powerful forces are shaking and remaking our world.

To renew America, we must be bold.

We have moved past the sterile debate between those who say government is the enemy and those who say government is the answer.

You must feel the winds of freedom blowing at your back, pushing you onward to a brighter future.

The real choice is whether we believe our best days are still out there or our best days are behind us.

So many of our problems do not stop at any nation's border.

May God strengthen our hands for the good work ahead.

We cannot ask Americans to be better citizens if we are not better servants.

*W*hen companies and workers work as a team they do better, and so does America.

We started as an experiment in democracy fueled by Europeans.

Let us remember that here on Earth, God's work must truly be our own.

Our children should grow up next to parks, not poison.

America has embodied an idea that has become the ideal for billions of people throughout the world.

For the very first time in all of history, more people on this planet live under democracy than dictatorship.

Big government does not have all the answers.

If we continue to be leaders for peace, then the next century can be the greatest time our Nation has ever known.

The barriers of the cold war are giving way to a global village where communication and cooperation are the order of the day.

We should do more to help new immigrants to fully participate in our community.

A society rooted in responsibility must provide safe streets, safe schools, and safe neighborhoods.

The common bonds of community which have been the great strength of our country from its very beginning are badly frayed.

It is time to support what works and stop supporting what doesn't.

You know one thing that's wrong with this country? Everybody gets a chance to have their fair say.

We need partners to build prosperity.

Guided by the ancient vision of a promised land, let us set our sights upon a land of new promise.

One of the greatest sources of our strength throughout the cold war was a bipartisan foreign policy.

We have to give the American people the tools they need to make the most of their God-given potential.

Our government, once a champion of national purpose, is now seen by many as simply a captive of narrow interests.

America saved the world from tyranny in two world wars and a long cold war.

It is so much easier to believe that our differences matter more than what we have in common. It is easier, but it is wrong.

We have to take advantage of progress to move closer to living as we say we believe.

America is making a difference for people here and around the world.

Growing connections of commerce and culture give us a chance to lift the fortunes and spirits of people the world over.

The will for peace is now stronger than the weapons of war.

We must keep our old democracy forever young.

If you read the Constitution, it's rooted in the desire to limit the Government's ability to mess with you.

For any one of us to succeed, we must succeed as one: America.

We should honor every legal immigrant here, working hard to be a good citizen, working hard to become a new citizen.

Engaging in honest dialogue is not an act of surrender, it is an act of strength and common sense.

America's security and prosperity require us to continue to lead in the world.

We need to do more to help disadvantaged people and distressed communities, no matter what their race or gender.

I intend to reclaim my family life for my family. It's nobody's business but ours.

Millions of Americans changed their own lives and put hate behind them. As a result, today all our lives are better.

Our great challenge for the 21st century is to find a way to be One America.

The American people have made our passage into the global information age an era of great American renewal.

We have to recognize that we cannot build our future without helping others to build theirs.

Let us remember . . . the first American Revolution was not won with a single shot; the continent was not settled in a single year.

The anger, the resentment, the bitterness . . .
they harden the heart and deaden the spirit
and lead to self-inflicted wounds.

Nothing big ever came from being small.

I don't seek to give anybody a guarantee, but I think
everybody ought to have a chance.

America has been a force for peace and prosperity
in every corner of the globe.

With a new century coming into view, old patterns are fading away: The cold war is gone; colonialism is gone; apartheid is gone.

It is time to end social promotion in America's schools.

We must have dramatic change in our economy, our government, and ourselves.

Those who work for peace have got to support one another.

*E*ducation no longer stops on graduation day.

*M*odern science has confirmed what ancient faiths have always taught: the most important fact of life is our common humanity.

*L*et us all take more responsibility, not only for ourselves and our families but for our communities and our country.

*W*e, all of us, will be judged by the dreams and deeds we pass on to our children.

We must have global vigilance.
And never again must we be shy
in the face of the evidence.

Hope is back in America. We are on the right track to the 21st century.

America must continue to be an unrelenting force for peace.

Each generation of Americans must define what it means to be an American.

No one wants to get this matter behind us more than I do—except maybe all the rest of the American people.

We must continue to see that science serves humanity, not the other way around.

Still today, too many of our police officers play by the rules of the bad old days.

Our founders gave us a democracy strong enough to endure for centuries, flexible enough to face our common challenges.

America must help more nations to break the bonds of disease.

The road to tyranny, we must never forget, begins with the destruction of the truth.

In an economy that honors opportunity, all Americans must be able to reap the rewards of prosperity.

America must look to the East no less than to the West.

We know that we are all in this together, that we are going to rise or fall together, that we have a duty to help each other.

*E*ach bloodletting hastens the next as the value of human life is degraded and violence becomes tolerated.

*O*ur rich texture of racial, religious and political diversity will be a Godsend in the 21st century.

*W*orking together, America has done well.

*P*eople all around the world look to America to be a force for peace and prosperity, freedom and security.

We have to root out the remnants of racism in our police departments.

In our times, America cannot and must not disentangle itself from the world.

America has good reason to work with Africa: 30 million Americans, more than one in ten, proudly trace their heritage here.

The same technological advances that have shrunk cell phones can also make weapons of terror easier to conceal and use.

I believe in religious liberty. I believe in freedom of speech. I believe in working hard and playing by the rules.

We have the best workers and the best products.

The real choice is whether we want a country of people all working together or one where you're on your own.

A shortsighted America will soon find its words falling on deaf ears all around the world.

There is an unbroken connection between the deeds of America's past and the daring of America's future.

How we fare as a nation far into the 21st century depends upon what we do as a nation today.

Europe's freedom and Europe's stability is vital to our own national security.

Global poverty is a powder keg that could be ignited by our indifference.

We must strengthen our gun laws and enforce those already on the books better.

Americans have ever been a restless, questing, hopeful people.

If you ever doubt whether the people are the boss in the end in a democracy, run for office.

Our nation's prosperity hasn't yet reached our inner cities, poor rural areas, and Native American reservations.

We have to be at the center of every vital global network, as a good neighbor and a good partner.

The world is divided according to how people believe they draw meaning from life.

A new season of American renewal has begun.

Democracy requires more than the insults and injustice and inequality that so many societies have known and America has known.

No child should be without a doctor just because a parent is without a job.

If America is to continue to lead the world, we must find the will to pay our way.

America again has the confidence to dream big dreams.

We can make college as universal in the 21st century as high school is today.

Our freedom and independence are actually enriched, not weakened, by our increasing interdependence with other nations.

We need a Europe that shares our values and shares the burdens of leadership.

If we want the world to embody our shared values, then we must assume a shared responsibility.

Often it's easier to believe that our differences matter more than what we have in common. It may be easier, but it's wrong.

I don't believe we should bet the farm, and I certainly don't believe we should bet the country.

To those who believe that God made each of us in His own image, how could we choose the darker road?

We remain the world's indispensable nation to advance prosperity, peace, and freedom and to keep our own children safe.

Our house is the greatest democracy in all human history.

It is time to break the bad habit of expecting something for nothing, from our government or from each other.

*We can't do everything,
   but we must do what we can.*

We must treat all our people with fairness and
  dignity, regardless of their race, religion, gender,
  or sexual orientation.

I misled people, including even my wife.
  I deeply regret that.

When Americans work together . . .
  they can meet any challenge.

Anyone contemplating any action that would
  endanger our troops should know this:
  America protects its own.

While more Americans are living better,
too many of our fellow citizens are working
harder just to keep up.

There are times when only America can make the
difference between war and peace.

I want every American to be able to hear those beautiful
words, "welcome home."

We must always marry our progress to the realization
of our values.

We have seen us grow stronger ... as we have given more and more of our people the chance to live their dreams.

The divide of race has been America's constant curse.

We must rise to the decisive moment, to make a nation and a world better than any we have ever known.

www.ingramcontent.com/pod-product-compliance
Lightning Source LLC
Chambersburg PA
CBHW061328040426
42444CB00011B/2821